LEARNING TOGETHER

IN THE

CHRISTIAN FELLOWSHIP

LEARNING TOGETHER IN THE CHRISTIAN FELLOWSHIP

BY SARA LITTLE

JOHN KNOX PRESS
Richmond, Virginia

Library of Congress Catalog Card Number: 56-9220

International Standard Book Number: 0-8042-1320-8

Fifteenth printing 1973

60-864-797

© JOHN KNOX PRESS 1956

Printed in the United States of America

Contents

Dick Smith:
Then, and Now

Dick Smith was the leader of a rather lifeless Sunday school class. He *was*, until one night when he listened as three of his friends discussed a study group to which they belonged in another church.

"I haven't studied so hard and thought so much since I was in school!" was the amazing statement made by one friend. Dick knew from experience that he could never depend upon more than one or two members of his class even to read the Sunday school lesson before coming to Sunday school.

"It's all so practical," said another. "I don't mean that anybody tells me to do this or not to do that—but somehow I feel that I get help in decisions I have to make on my job, and in my home. It really makes a difference in my understanding of what it means to live the Christian life." Dick had often wondered whether his teaching really helped those who were in his class.

"What I like," the third friend said, "is the fact that

7

members of our group seem to care genuinely for one another. I even feel that, if I need help in any way, I could get it from members of that group."

Today, Dick Smith is still the teacher of the same people, but his class is a different class. Members seem reluctant to miss, when they have to be away. They study at home before the class meets, and have occasional extra "bull sessions." Old members have brought in new members until leaders are considering the question of whether the class should be divided. Dick himself has changed, too, both as a person and as a teacher. The process of "ups and downs" (because it was not so smooth and automatic as might appear on the surface!) has been—and will continue to be—the opportunity for real growth in both Dick and other class members.

Obviously, what happened took longer than two weeks! In fact, the conversation that was overheard by Dick was but the beginning.

The next Sunday Dick told his class about the other study group, and immediately someone suggested that a special committee be appointed to visit the study group to find out more. The committee was appointed and soon decided to visit the other study group for four weeks to see if they could learn "some new ways of doing things." Since the study group in the other church met on Wednesday nights Dick decided to join the committee in its visits.

When the committee reported back to the class on the next Sunday, they confirmed the fact that something was happening, but professed ignorance as to why because they had not seen much that was different from the ways in which Dick sometimes taught the lesson. The materials used were exactly the same, and the methods only slightly different. They reported further, however, that the committee had arranged for a meeting with the leaders of the other group, and so they hoped to be able to report more on a future Sunday.

The next Sunday, the committee chairman reported again, but this time he stated that the conference with leaders of the class had been most helpful. He explained that these leaders told of how the whole group had some months before become concerned about itself and resolved to study the question of what a study group in the church was supposed to be and do. The group had hoped to find suggestions of "new ways of doing things" but the study had taken them much further, and now "ways of doing things" seemed simply something to be used in achieving the much more basic purposes of the church. They had learned that the church needs to provide people with a kind of fellowship in which they can feel that their needs are respected and in which the whole group seeks to help them with their needs. The leaders had explained that it was their desire to create this kind of fellowship which had led them to the use of certain methods in which each person participated and felt that he was a member in every way.

The committee chairman, then, reported that the committee had decided to recommend that the class begin as soon as possible a study of the place of study groups, such as Sunday school classes, in the whole program of the church.

The class, by this time, had heard enough to be interested and so such a study was begun. The class studied carefully the meaning of learning in a group, the way to use methods so that the whole group actually studies, the special applications of this to Bible study, and the implications of this study for the work of the church.

The results are now being realized in the class of which Dick Smith *is* still the teacher. The members of his class are now making statements similar to the ones overheard by Dick as he listened to the conversation of his friends. And next week a visiting committee from another class has asked Dick to meet with it to tell them about "some new ways of doing things."

As Dick spoke to his wife about this approaching meeting with the committee of the other class, he said, "I'm going to talk with them about *learning together in the Christian fellowship,* of course."

Many persons in the church of today are called to Christian service as the leaders of study groups. Some, like Dick Smith, are called to teach classes of the Sunday church school; some to serve as the leaders of special study groups for men, women, mixed adults, young adults, older adults, students, and youth; some to serve as the leaders of special study groups created for leadership education and for parent education purposes.

All of these are called to help the participants in such

groups to learn together in the Christian fellowship, which is the church.

At least four basic questions should become the concern of all who are called to such service, and so this booklet tries to suggest some of the ideas which may provide help for those who need to formulate answers to these four questions:

First — *Is group study a vital way to help persons grow in Christian knowledge and develop in Christian maturity? If so, why, and under what conditions?* Basic theological and educational presuppositions are involved, and those who seek to lead groups in study without formulating a satisfactory answer to these questions may be building upon sand.

Second — *How does one lead group members to participate purposefully and effectively in study?* That is to say, *how can a leader utilize various methods to achieve specific purposes?*

Third — *What does this mean, specifically, for Bible study?* The Bible is basic for Christian faith and life, and so it is essential that the implications of answers to the preceding questions be considered in relation to Bible study.

Fourth — *What are the implications for the church's program and for the kind of leadership required for it?* Satisfactory group study must be based on sound planning and preparation, upon a willingness on the part of participants and leaders to accept their responsibilities in such study, and upon the maintenance of a satisfactory relationship between the group and the church as a whole.

These four questions are considered in the four major divisions of this booklet. The answers suggested are not final ones. They are intended to stimulate further thought, investigation, and experimentation. The answers suggested are offered with an earnest hope that all who read will refuse to use methods simply as gadgets, but all the while will be seeking to become more seriously aware of our Christian heritage and of the implications of our faith for the way we do things.

We Learn, Together

Members of the Christian Church are becoming increasingly sensitive to a need for more knowledge of the Bible, of Church history, and of Christian beliefs. They are attending church activities in increasing numbers and are demanding study materials which will provide them with the kind of information they seek.

Because of these demands, the leaders of church activities sometimes become confused as they try to provide what people want, and turn to the use of materials and procedures which become even less satisfying in the end.

The Christian faith cannot be really learned, cannot have its full meaning so long as it is no more than acquiring factual knowledge, or verbalizing freely about Christian doctrine. This has rarely been said better than John Calvin said it more than four hundred years ago.

> Doctrine is not an affair of the tongue, but of the life . . . is received only when it possesses the whole soul, and finds its seat and habitation in the inmost recesses of the heart. . . . To

doctrine in which our religion is contained we have given the first place, since by it our salvation commences; but it must be transfused into the breast, and pass into the conduct, and so transform us into itself, as not to prove unfruitful.[1]

Is it really possible to "teach" this kind of vital Christianity—a knowledge that makes a difference *in* people and *to* people, where they live? Perhaps the "teaching" that will be most effective in the development of such a faith will be a "learning together," as people study that which seems important to them, and as they help one another through groups that are real fellowships, changing and sustaining those who participate in them. Perhaps group study does offer an avenue by which persons may move toward both knowledge and maturity.

THE INDIVIDUAL AND THE GROUP

Let us turn first, therefore, to notice the nature of the group in which learning can take place. One might say that in recent years sociologists, psychologists, psychiatrists, personnel specialists, educators, and others have rediscovered "groups" and their importance to individuals. On every hand, today, there is an increasing recognition of the fact that an individual needs to have an opportunity to become a responsible, active participant in some group which will accept him fully, if he is to find adequate security and fulfillment.

It has been pointed out, for example, that during the war, prisoners or displaced persons were able to "hold together" as persons chiefly because they were identified with a group that was sharing the same experience.[2] The same power of the group may be seen today in the voluntary Alcoholics Anonymous. Some churches have found ways to set up groups — primarily for therapeutic purposes—through which members help one another as they try to find ways of meeting their personal problems. A point to be considered is that, at least in part, already existing groups may come to serve this same kind of purpose, of promoting mental health, as is pointed out in the next section of this chapter.

The rapid rise of adult education groups, sponsored by a variety of public agencies, indicates a recognition of the value of the group for the whole process of study and learning. Educators believe that real learning occurs when persons are caught up in the dynamic currents of group thinking. They have found, for example, that persons learn best when they *work* at it—when they are encouraged to think, to question, to verbalize their understanding of a fact or situation. As individuals in a group stimulate one another in thinking, cause one another to do individual study outside the group, bring new insights into the total picture, revise their formulations of ideas, they acquire more knowledge because they have actively participated in the learning situation. Of course mere activity, verbal or otherwise, is not enough. Purposeful and real participation is essential.

The impact of the group upon the individual goes beyond acquisition of knowledge to change of attitudes. John

Powell, speaking out of much experience in informal adult education, has this to say:

> The artless testimony of changing attitudes is familiar to all who have worked with genuine groups. From my own recent groups, I think of three men: the press writer who remarked, "This is changing the *way* I think. I've begun to listen to myself the same way I do to other people"; the Southerner who remarked, after a sharp but amicable argument over race relations, "Matter of fact, this is the first time I ever sat at the same table with a Negro"—and shook hands with his opponent; and, to me the most significant, an Army colonel who had begun the year contentious and disputatious and who interjected in a later discussion, "I still don't think I agree with you, but I no longer care just about beating your argument. *You see something I don't, and I want to understand it.*"[3]

Others who have been studying in the field of "group dynamics" have helped us to see that within any group are forces which vitally influence a person's growth and behavior—the group-climate, the part a person plays in the group (his role and status), the constant interaction among group members. These forces have a great deal to do with what a person learns and the kind of person he becomes.

The conclusions of many writers and the experiences of specialists in many fields seem to say clearly that, for good or ill, the group does something to the individual (just as the individual in part determines the nature of the group).

THE "REDEEMING" COMMUNITY

We must now ask, "What does this have to say to the church?"

There are many groups in the church. Sometimes these groups are genuine fellowship through which the grace of God can reach the participants, casting out fears, healing wounds, and giving purpose and direction for life. But such groups are all too rare. Far more often one finds groups in which most persons engage in activities in a spectator capacity, rather than as a participant understanding and sharing in the purposes of the activities. A person can be lost in the crowd in a large church, known by a few other people and addressed politely but only superficially by most. A person can be exploited by the church in being urged to participate in activities to make them "successful" rather than to find help for himself. Occasionally he may be vaguely stirred by hearing an interpretation of the message of a prophet, or by an elusive idea that almost touches him. But nothing *real* happens. Too concerned about himself and what people think of him to be interested in those other people, sometimes desiring to communicate with others about the central issues of life and yet not knowing how to begin, he moves on, lonely in the midst of many people and anxious about something, he knows not what. One writer has said,

> Our communities and churches are filled with frightened and lonely people who, being afraid to give themselves in personal encounter, seek solace in the comfort of things, only to suffer from an increased sense of estrangement and death.[4]

When the sense of security and fulfillment so necessary to human beings is found more through participation in secular groups than in church groups, it is time for the church to be troubled. Many people are finding in non-church groups an atmosphere which warms and accepts them, in a way that makes them experience something akin to the love they hear defined in the church. One leader who studied in the Great Books discussion groups states that "the creation of an atmosphere of understanding and acceptance is basic for learning to take place and be assimilated."[5] She sees certain implications for the church. The understanding and acceptance of which public educators and group work agencies speak are, in the church, love and forgiveness. Rejection may be equated with judgment on the human level.

Acceptance may be necessary for learning to take place —but Christian love and forgiveness that should be characteristic of the church bear within them a power which points to God and His redemption, a power which may sustain that individual who responds in faith to the love of God, revealed to him through the fellowship of the church.

It is, therefore, within the church that a person might hope to experience *koinonia,* that fellowship, that sense of community binding Christians together—a fellowship which is, indeed, far more than a sense of "groupness." Baillie says that God's eternal purpose for man was that he might be a part of this fellowship, and that, through the fellowship, he might become what God intended him to be.

In such a "fellowship of persons united in the love of God," men would become as "one body," free but not individualistic, and knowing the truth that "fellowship with God and fellowship with men cannot be separated in human life—can hardly even be distinguished."[6]

Has man become a part of that "one body"? The answer is obvious. Man's sin, in putting himself in the center of the universe where God ought to be, Baillie says, has separated him from both God and his fellow men. He adds,

> But God has never given mankind up. He has always had His purpose. And (so far as we can venture to describe the divine plan in human history) His method of saving mankind has been like this. Thousands of years ago He started a new community, a little one at first, in order that it might be the nucleus of a new mankind. . . . they would find their own salvation in being used for the salvation of mankind. Thus they would be a redeemed and redeeming community, through which all the world would be drawn back out of its disintegration into the life of community with God and man, and so the nucleus would grow into a new mankind.[7]

Israel failed. It was only as God was in Christ reconciling the world unto Himself and creating the "Community of the Cross" that His divine plan for saving mankind continued to work.

And it is the Church, the spiritual Israel, the Body of Christ, made into a new community through the indwelling presence of the Holy Spirit, which carries on the work of reconciliation.

. . . About the Mission of the Church

In what way is this related to study groups? Perhaps several observations will help clarify this matter.

Study groups carried on within the framework of the church, whether in the church building itself, on the college campus, or in the neighborhood, can justify their existence only in so far as they share in the church's work of fulfilling God's eternal purpose for mankind.

Transformation of personality occurs as men meet God, who in His grace seeks them in their lostness and aloneness. Indeed, drawing them to Him, away from their self-love and inadequacies, God enables them to become "a new creation." It is only through the supporting power of that quality of life provided by the Christian group that this transformation can take place. As man changes, he moves toward Christian maturity. And is not this, in part, what is meant by the doctrine of sanctification?

Those who experience this new relationship with God and with one another, this sense of being made whole, feel an inner compulsion to help others discover in their own lives the power of God's redemptive love. Because they are themselves free, they can accept new ideas, meet hostilities, and care for unlovely people. Because they do not speak in abstract terms, but can witness (testify) to the things they know to be true, because of what by God's grace they have become and are becoming, they can reach all manner of people.

It has been suggested that where missionaries can find no point of contact between systems of thought, there *is* a point of contact between *people;* thus it is only in personal community, not in the mind of one individual, that the breach between different groups can be crossed, as Christians and non-Christians "learn to hold together in personal groups of love and sympathy and patience."[8]

For the college campus, this is a way of witnessing to the intellectual, to the person confused and troubled by contemporary events, to the agnostic. For any group, it is a way of cutting across social barriers. Surely this is one form of evangelism.

. . . About the Way God Confronts Man

Much that has been said about the mission of the Church, and, earlier, about God's purpose and plan for saving mankind, is relevant here. Several other thoughts may be helpful.

The whole story of God's dealing with man is a record of His working with the individual in community. There is a new awareness, these days, that salvation is not a transaction between one individual and God, carried on without relation to or concern for other people. Biblical scholars point out that a person's salvation comes to him, in part, as a member of a group; this is true in the New Testament as well as in the Old, for "even here the individual is never thought of as being saved entirely by himself apart from the community of the saved."[9]

God is the God of history. He does not detach Himself from the world of men, waiting to be found by them; rather, He seeks them, confronting them in the midst of their experiences. The Bible is the drama of God at work in history, leading men in crisis and in everyday occurrences to interpret their experiences in the light of their faith. Thus He reveals Himself. The creative interaction of men, struggling together to hear what God says in the events of today, becomes a medium by which He continues to confront them.

God's ultimate revelation is that of a Person speaking to persons. God incarnate in Jesus Christ, the "Word made flesh," spoke and speaks to man in act and in Being. Somehow, when a person meets Jesus Christ, all that he is and does speaks to other men of this Christ—and enables them to meet Him, too. It is not one area of life that is touched, but the whole person. All that he is stands in awe before all that Christ is—and he is redeemed.

The Holy Spirit creates that kind of community in which the truth can be communicated. Men need feel no pride in their own accomplishment when it is evident that a truly redemptive community has come alive. This cannot happen without their full and free response to God's seeking love, it is true, but it is the Holy Spirit who creates real fellowship—*koinonia.* Here it is that the "language of relationship," as well as the "language of words," can exist.

This is what I call the language of relationship, the communication that results from living together and which gives us the basic and personal meanings for the words we hear and use. The spirit of the relationship determines the nature of the communication. . . . The Holy Spirit, Who brings into *being* the fellowship of love and reconciliation through that same relationship, provides the experiences that cause us to *become reconciled* and to *be reconcilers.*[10]

. . . About Man's Response to God

Every man who hears and answers God's call to him becomes a part of the Body of Christ, participating in the life of an organism in which the abilities of each one are needed by all members of that organism. This love and concern, this bearing of one another's burdens, is in a real sense a part of the ministry of the Church—a ministry shared by laymen and clergy alike—and recalls the doctrine of the "priesthood of all believers" as a "profound Christian truth," which is ignored "at peril of personal and ecclesiastical sickness." It is, indeed, "one essential condition of being a Christian."[11]

Ross Snyder interprets this doctrine of the priesthood of all believers by reference to Martin Luther's instructions to Christians to act "reciprocally and mutually one the Christ of the other, doing to our neighbor as Christ does to us," and "to put on our neighbor."

> "To put on our neighbor" means that all the resources of our life are available to our neighbor—the way we see and feel, our ideas, achievements, relationships, love, power, faith. Further we put on the way he sees and feels the world, his sorrows, sins, anxieties and frustrations. We deal with them as if they were our own.[12]

But man responds to God, not just by being a responsible member of the Christian community; he responds by becoming the person God intended him to be. (In a way, of course, the two are the same thing.) He does not cater to people to win their favor, nor state his beliefs to fit conventional expectations. Knowing himself to be loved, he loves; knowing himself to be understood, he understands. There is an inner integrity, a courageous honesty about him. Realizing his own sinfulness, he opens himself to change, and disciplines himself to learn from others and to make himself available to them. Thus he becomes himself.

. . . About the Learning, Redeeming Community

All that has been said applies to the life and work of the Christian Church as a whole. Yet it applies equally to any particular group of Christians — for the Church exists wherever a small group is gathered; to two or three gathered in the name of Christ, the Spirit of truth is promised. (Matthew 18:19-20.) It seems clear that what is sought by the Church is not a collection of creeds, an acquisition of verbalizations—although the ability to state one's faith is desirable—but an "education into religion,"[13] where a man's religion becomes the controlling power of his life.

This will happen when groups set up to "teach" religion become "person-oriented" as well as "task-oriented." That is to say, it will be remembered that people bring to groups "hidden agendas" stemming from their fears and failures and need for acceptance and security. This means that, while there will be an effort to cover content, to present a good program, to perform a task, there will also be a conscious awareness that every person is an individual of dignity and worth, capable of sharing in the making of decisions and setting of goals, of accepting responsibility, of facing the consequences of acts, of evaluating their experiences as an aid to growth toward intellectual, spiritual, and emotional maturity. This will happen, too, when groups become fellowships with members sharing in a mutuality of concern and purpose, when they begin to see knowledge and experience interwoven into real learning that eventuates in a way of life.

GROUP STUDY: VALUES AND DANGERS

What, in brief summary, are some of the values of group study for the Christian fellowship?

First, it offers a valid way for men to learn the content and relevance of the Christian religion. What person, having struggled to articulate a belief in a way that others could understand, has not found himself with a firmer grasp on the reality of that belief? Who, having met opposition, has not been grateful for the necessity to sharpen and clarify an idea? Who, having been stimulated and challenged by the shared insights of another person, has not seen a whole new world open up before him?

Second, it offers a valid approach to the *particular kind* of learning necessitated by the nature of the Christian faith. That is to say, truth is communicated through persons, through what they are and how they act, as well as through words and ideas. People not only learn facts— they change. The group itself becomes a channel for God's work of redemption.

Third, the Christian group can so sustain an individual that he no longer faces the world alone. His learning achieves a permanence it would not otherwise have. His new way of life is rooted in a fellowship which upholds that way. The "priesthood of believers" becomes a reality.

Fourth, this approach would seem to be consistent theologically with the Christian understanding of the mission of the Church, of the way God confronts man and man responds to God.

Obviously, and unfortunately, what has been said refers to that which exists only potentially and partially. This kind of thing can and does become a reality only through persons who know their dependence on God and their responsibility before Him.

There are some dangers and difficulties to be mentioned, also.

First, it is dangerous to assume that group study will automatically produce changed persons—or, even, that it is the only approach to people. Unless people really study individually as well, they may have nothing to contribute after a while. They "pool ignorance," as someone has said, or engage in "intellectual ping pong."[14] Unless they follow through with deep thinking, and work out their own pattern for the interrelationship of ideas, their learning is not intellectually respectable.

Leaders may mistakenly assume progress when they see people active or talkative. This "misplaced participation," says one modern writer, may be found in business where extreme care is taken to work for high morale by consulting and planning with all levels of workers in what is often only a gesture to make them think they have a part in decisions; this, he says, may be merely busywork. Certainly it involves "enforced sociability." Along with this goes what he calls "false personalization." When there is a "spurious and effortful glad hand" by managers compelled by the system in which they work to be "sold on the superior values of personalization," there results a personalization that is false because of its "compulsory and manipulatory character."[15]

This same "false personalization" can occur when *too much* emphasis is placed on the "person-oriented" group. People can become themselves only when they are freed by looking toward something outside themselves, bigger than they are. The intrinsic value of the content to be studied, or the task to be accomplished, must challenge them. Too much subjectivity can lead to morbidity.

All of this represents an extreme, of course. So long as people's concern for one another is genuine, rooted in Christian love, and so long as they are persons of integrity, the kind of danger indicated here will be avoided.

A *second* danger is that there may develop too much emphasis on the group process. Because there are certain procedures which seem to result in better participation and more interest than others, these procedures may be employed indiscriminately, without adequate reference either to their appropriateness for the occasion or to their suitability for the content being considered. They may, in fact, become ends in themselves, and a person may almost feel compelled to use certain methods, more because they are "fashionable" than because they can accomplish desired goals. Even informality in leadership may become an end in itself. (And an artificial informality is more amusing than helpful!)

This does not mean to say that people are to avoid knowing about methods, and mastering their use; rather, it is to emphasize the importance of knowing the *why* behind them, and then of using them wisely.

A *third* danger may develop when there is too much emphasis on the importance of the group. A part of the current trend is a swing away from an overemphasis on individualism. Living in a culture which develops people who desperately need social approval, the church may unintentionally allow the group (rather than the truth as communicated through the group) to become the determining influence on the lives of its members. When people become "other-directed," they feel guilty, not about failure to live up to inner standards, but about failure to be popular, or to manage smoothly their relations with other people.[16]

Obviously, if a person says "I believe . . ." in order to secure approval, or uses certain words to arouse admiration, he is defeating the whole purpose of what has been projected as an opportunity for Christian growth. The quality of life in a group is determined by the people who compose the group. It matters a great deal, therefore, who and what the members of the group are; a redeeming minority must be present. It matters a great deal that the goal is not to develop "other-directed" people, but people whose lives are directed by their Christian faith.

Somehow, responsible persons must keep a total and balanced perspective in view. For it must never be forgotten that the person is a unique self. In the final analysis, the person stands alone, with depths not encompassed by any group.

Indeed, it is *because* of this—because man becomes a person, a self, only as an *individual in community*—that the Christian group, avoiding the pitfalls and actualizing the potentialities, is here conceived of as an instrument for the fulfilling of God's purpose for man.

We Participate, While Learning

Thinking about the learning, redeeming community, gaining a vision of what it is like, is a very necessary first step if study groups in a church are to be vital. Unless there be a consciousness of the significance of groups and their possibilities, leaders are not likely to improve those now existing, or to set up new ones to fill new purposes. But gaining such a vision is only a first step.

If a leader concludes that group study is valuable in helping people to grow in Christian knowledge and maturity, he must then seek to understand how one can lead a group to provide for purposeful and effective participation.

Think again about what happened to Dick Smith (as related on pages 7-10).

First, he developed a purpose, one that was his own. He wanted certain things to happen in that Sunday school class. Second, he put forth some effort to find out what he could do about the matter—and he and the class started to work. Third, he evaluated what was happening in the

31

class, alone and with the members. It was work—rewarding work, to be sure, but work, nevertheless. And something happened in Dick's group.

These are the same things that must characterize any learning situation if the individual is to get the greatest good from the group. A person must understand and share in the purpose, he must put forth effort in study, and he must work to make the group the best group possible, evaluating the group's progress and his part in it.

PURPOSE AND LEARNING

We must now turn to the close relationship between purpose and learning if we are to understand the methods to be used in leading a group.

Unless a person *wants* to learn, unless something makes a difference to him, unless he has a purpose which helps to determine what he accepts as his own, the things which happen will remain *outside* of him. He must become involved, or participate, at the level of purpose. When this happens, then his purpose becomes an inner motivation to learn, generating a power within him to put forth effort to become a responsible group member.

The purpose may not be there to begin with. It was not, with Dick Smith. It was only as the casual talk with his friends moved along that his purpose developed. If a person enters a group, even one with ready-made purposes or with a purposeless existence following conventional patterns, it is possible for his interest to be awakened. Then, as he helps shape the direction in which the group moves, as he sees the relevance to his life of the truths discussed, his purposes develop and coincide with group purposes. Occasional opportunities for the group to articulate its purpose, and to evaluate progress, will help, of course.

It is interesting to observe that many of the procedures to be suggested under methods of study are equally well adapted for use in planning and evaluation, so that group members may have opportunities to express or modify purposes, and to make decisions regarding the functioning of the group.

METHODS OF STUDY

Method in itself communicates content. That is to say, the *way* something is approached in part determines what is learned, as well as whether it is learned. Consider Mr. Sadler. No matter how many times he repeats his pet phrases concerning the worth and dignity of man, the fact that he always lectures, dogmatically and in a detached voice, with his eye on the lefthand ceiling of the room, has meant that what he really is teaching is the exact reverse of the words he uses. Method does teach, in itself. And the method used has a great deal to do with the atmosphere of a group, with group interrelationships, and therefore is directly related to some of the intangible but basic learning and change that take place in persons.

Even though these things be true, methods cannot be chosen arbitrarily. It is not possible to take number one from the current listing of "best" methods. A method is "best" *only* as it "belongs" to that subject matter and that purpose which it can help to bring alive as it is used with wisdom by leaders. As methods are suggested here, therefore, there are four points to serve as reminders to group leaders.

1. Methods are to be chosen for their appropriateness to purpose, content, ages, and characteristics of group members, and time available. (For example, it would be rather absurd to try role-playing and buzz groups in a twenty-minute period. Or to suggest pasting pictures in a notebook to college students.)

2. Use of a variety of methods can help a leader to maintain interest in a group. But appropriateness should always take precedence over variety. Never should a leader try to use all of the methods he can use in any *one* study session! It is to be recalled, too, that effective use of methods for group study involves certain skills on the part of group members—not just mastery on the part of the leader. Occasionally, therefore, a group may have to stop and study a method directly, in order to be able to use it successfully.

3. When methods are conceived of as ways to help in opening channels of communication between individuals, freeing them to contribute and to benefit from contributions of others, they become something more than "techniques to secure participation." Or, rather, they become ways of helping make participation possible on a level that is deep and real. Actually, they

are simply ways in which people work together—whether in planning committees, in study groups, in action groups. Although many people think of teaching in a more formal way, with emphasis on content-to-be-covered, it is nevertheless true that many teachers would find these ways the most natural and logical ways to work with classes. It is considered here, therefore, that the teacher of a Sunday school class may serve as the group leader, just as, in voluntary study groups, any member may serve as leader, or there may be a rotating leadership. Whatever the situation, it is always true that *all* members of a group are responsible for its success or failure—not just the leader.

4. The physical arrangement of the room has much to do with the effectiveness of methods. If possible, it is well for the group to sit in a circle or semicircle, or around a table. (In most study groups there will probably be ten to fifteen persons.) The leader sits somewhere in the circle, not behind a special table. A movable chalkboard is a help.

Methods explained here may suggest other ideas about ways that will help make it possible for people to communicate with one another. Some idea of the relative values of various types of methods of study may be gained from the chart[1] included here, although the chart is called "Checklist of Program Methods." These are, as has been suggested before, simply "ways in which people work together."

Checklist

of

Program

Methods

METHOD

Lecture, film, reading, recitals, etc.

Forum

Symposium panel or debate

Discussion

Project, field trip, exhibits, etc.

"Buzz groups"

Group interview

Reprinted from *Adult Leadership*, monthly publication of the Adult Education Association of the U. S. A.

CHIEF CHARACTERISTIC	PATTERN OF PARTICIPATION	SPECIAL USEFULNESS	LIMITATIONS
rmation-giving.		Systematic presentation of knowledge.	Little opportunity for audience to participate.
rmation giving owed by questions clarification.		Audience can obtain the specific information it wants on particular aspects of the subject.	Formality; lack of freedom to interchange ideas.
sentation of differ- points of view.		Different points of view spotlight issues, approaches, angles; stimulate analysis.	Can get off the beam; personality of speakers may overshadow content: vocal speaker or questioner can monopolize program.
h degree of group ticipation.		Pooling of ideas, experience, and knowledge; arriving at group decisions.	Practical with only a limited number of people.
stigation of a blem cooperatively.	PROBLEM	Gives first-hand experience.	Requires extra time and energy for planning.
% participation by e audiences ugh small clusters participants.		Makes individual discussion, pooling of ideas, possible in large groups. Develops leadership skill in members.	Contributions are not likely to be very deep or well organized.
ntaneous giving of ions and facts by erts in response to stions.		Brings knowledge from a number of sources to bear on one problem.	Becomes disorganized without careful planning of material to be covered.

Buzz Groups

Used in an almost endless variety of ways, the division of a group into smaller sub-groups for a limited period of time with a specific thing to be done can be one of the best ways to help a person enter and become a part of the group. Six is the usual number (originally called Phillips 66, because Dr. Phillips of Michigan State College started the practice of dividing an audience into groups of six for six minutes), but in small groups two people may constitute a buzz group. Chairs can be quickly separated into small groupings, one row of persons can turn and face another in groups of four or six, or other arrangements can be quickly worked out. Amazingly enough, the "buzz" of voices does not seem disconcerting, even in a crowded room.

Some simple device may be employed for securing a leader of the buzz group. The one whose last name begins with the first letter of the alphabet may be asked to start things going, or the tallest person in the group, or the one who traveled the greatest distance. If a secretary or reporter is needed, some other device may be used to secure that person, or the discussion starter may designate someone to serve. Often only one person is needed—and often no plan is needed to start the discussion, but the leader emerges from the group.

What are some of the possibilities? At the beginning of a new unit, have each buzz group list one thing they want to learn during the study, or raise one question they want answered, or list one thing they already know about the subject. Before a speech, let a buzz group list one question they hope to have answered; re-group after the speech to see whether and how the question was answered. After a speech, let each group raise a question they would like to ask the speaker; group representatives then gather to question the speaker. If a passage is being studied, ask each group to read it silently and discuss the answer to a specific question—either the same question for all groups, or a different question for each sub-group. Or each group may raise one question for further discussion by the total group. A unit summary can well be developed through the use of buzz groups, with each group listing one or two of the most important facts learned, or attitudes changed, or other results. An imaginative leader could go on indefinitely; he would need only to beware of the danger of overusing this productive method.

Work Groups

Work groups, like buzz groups, result from the division of a group into smaller sub-groups. Of about the same size as buzz groups, work groups stay together for longer periods of time and their work is broader in scope, allowing for more concentrated thinking.

When the leader of one Bible study group on a college campus wanted to stimulate interest in Philippians and get a quick preview of what people knew and wanted to know, he gave three small groups five minutes to raise one question each. This was the buzz group. Another leader presented certain background material for orientation, discussed the salutation and its meaning, and then asked each group to study Philippians 1:3-11 with the aim of writing in one sentence the heart of the message of that passage. After twenty minutes, each group presented its sentence, and a general comparison and discussion followed. This was a work group.

Sometimes a work group takes even longer. It may collect information, or organize and interpret it. It may do outside investigation. Sometimes one group presents a report dramatically, another as a panel, another as an interview with two of its members participating. The group leader may need to work in advance with leaders of work groups; often this is not necessary. When the job to be done is clearly understood, and when members know how to study together, the work group gives a real opportunity for every member of a group to "dig in."

Group Discussion

Conversation is often mistakenly called discussion. Real group discussion presupposes preparation on the part of the members, who are aware of the need for disciplined and purposeful thinking, and who are willing to work to improve their skills in co-operative efforts to solve some problem, to arrive at some decision, or to come to some understanding.

No two discussions are alike, and there is no rigid pattern to be followed, but it may be helpful to look at three steps which are frequently found in a discussion.

1. The statement of the subject to be discussed.

Many times people do not address their remarks to the subject because they are not sure what they are discussing. After giving a brief background or explanation, or an introduction designed to arouse immediate interest, the leader may wish to state in *one sentence or one question* exactly what is to be discussed. It may need to be modified. Its limitations may need to be stated. But people can work better when they know what they are discussing—and when the subject is one suitable to be approached through the discussion method (as many subjects are not).

2. The discussion proper.
    A good leader would work out a discussion pattern in advance, but would be willing and able to modify it. He would have some plan for getting the discussion started, and some idea of the pattern of development it might follow. For example, to aid in orderly movement, he might wish to list questions on a chalkboard, and then follow the listing; or he might wish to list major areas—as "issues involved," "available facts," "possible solutions," "obstacles"—to serve as a guide. Always listening to people and respecting them, seeking to make it possible for all to contribute and none to monopolize, he would sometimes rephrase questions, sometimes stop for a brief summary and restatement of the goal.

3. Summary and conclusion.
    If it is possible to do so, it is well to state the conclusion

at which the group seems to have arrived, in a way satisfactory to them. But often no real agreement has been reached, and there will be a summary of progress and a statement of unsolved issues. Many times this final statement is unnecessary. A small group where members have met and worked together for a long time might find a verbalized statement an objectionable rehashing of what they knew. A sensitive leader, however, will know when to summarize and state conclusions, or when to end a session in some other way.

A general discussion often includes many types of discussion within one session—buzz groups, panels, question and answer periods—or combines with other types of study procedures. This means that a good discussion leader is not only flexible, but is a person of great resourcefulness. Such qualifications would reveal themselves in at least two ways: the leader would be familiar with and skilled in the use of many aids to discussion, and he would be sensitive to individuals within the group.

There are innumerable aids to discussion which are especially valuable in getting started, or in stimulating new interest when attention seems to lag. The use of a brief unfinished story, or a dramatization or a tape recording, or a case study—any of these can prove of value. One study guide suggests two other ideas. The first is that of using a problem census.

Before the group adjourns, do a problem census. Distribute 3 x 5" cards to each person. Ask each member to write on one side of the card his answer to this question:

Of the many social problems presented in the Report on "The Responsible Society," what problem do you believe is of greatest concern to Christians in this community?

On the other side of the card, each group member answers this question:

As a responsible Christian and a member of this church, what would you want the church to do about this problem?

Collect the cards and tabulate the answers on a blackboard. Many of them can be grouped for similarity.[2]

A second idea is that of using an opinionnaire.

In each question or statement, check the phrase that seems to describe *most accurately your opinion* or understanding of the issue.

1. Apathy to social issues is due principally to:
   ......a. inadequate instruction in the Bible and Christian theology.
   ......b. lack of information and understanding of public issues.
   ......c. belief that religion and politics do not mix.
   ......d. sense of hopelessness and futility of individual efforts.

2. Christians can work *most effectively* for a responsible society by:
   ......a. concentrating on the salvation of souls.
   ......b. conscientious study of present-day issues and urging their public officials to take these issues seriously.
   ......c. working faithfully in the political party of their choice.[3]

Use of both the problem census and the multiple-choice opinionnaire or questionnaire will help stimulate interest and raise issues that need consideration. Another idea that may help if a group is stymied, or contributions seem to be pious or prosaic, or members tend to sit in judgment on each other, is "brainstorming," a term coined by Alex Osborn in *Your Creative Power.*

> Its procedure is simple. Rules of judgment are suspended, if only temporarily. A problem is posed. For a period of ten or fifteen minutes the members of the committee or audience are urged to put forward their most ridiculous ideas. These are recorded without comment and without criticism. Criticism is reserved. . . . And the practice of letting the creative imagination run riot without the usual shushing restraints tends to loosen up the group, to encourage suggestions, and to foster a spirit that cannot possibly develop in any other way.[4]

Business has used the idea to improve insurance policies and to manufacture new erasers. Program planning groups have dealt with subjects for meetings, titles for speeches, publicity plans. We are advised that "brainstorming works best when it is applied to really difficult problems,"[5] and that it provides a means of getting to the spontaneous ideas on people's minds.

Sometimes students have real questions about doctrinal beliefs, or interpretations of Bible incidents, and think the questions are too absurd to be mentioned. Freed from the possibility of being criticized, they may bring out into the open vital questions or new insights. What is not good can be discarded when the group gets back to a more reasoned discussion—and members will have enjoyed the experience.

No matter what plan is followed to aid in the movement of a discussion, it is doomed to failure unless the leader knows how to use carefully worded questions. There are ways of helping persons be specific and clear in their thinking. There are ways of helping a whole group to see where it stands and to work together with maximum effectiveness. There would be questions like "Why?" and "How?" and "Such as. . . ?" Or, "Is this what you're saying?" and "It seems to you that . . ." And there would be "Is this what we've said so far?" or "What is our next step?" A casual observer, looking in on a group where a good discussion leader is at work, hearing only his brief questions and comments, would doubtless be entirely unaware of the concentrated effort demanded, a labor that is mentally exhausting, but that enables him to know when questions are needed to bring forth more information, or indicate relation of facts, or to stimulate deeper inquiry into issues involved.

The need for the leader to be sensitive to individuals within the group has already been mentioned. One person, having heard that wide participation was desirable, said to a shy member, "Mary, you haven't said anything today. Do you know the answer to this question?" It was a factual question, and Mary did not know the answer. The leader had violated Mary's right *not* to speak, and had embarrassed her. Had the leader felt that Mary *wanted* to speak, and only needed a slight encouragement, he might have said, "Yesterday we were talking about . . . Your idea comes in right at this point, Mary. Want to tell the group about it?"

He might use some other plan. Usually, it is better to address questions, especially factual ones, to the group as a whole, rather than to individuals. When a member begins talking too much, the leader can summarize what he has said, and ask for someone else's opinion, or he can say, "I see . . . I believe we have an idea over here." Only rarely would he deliberately say, "Bill, why don't you give somebody else a chance to talk?" Of course it is impossible to say what words or expressions to use and what not to use, because the tone of one's voice often determines what is really communicated. The leader whose genuine interest in people springs from his basic Christian motivation will know what to say and do; there are no rules to follow, but there is an attitude which finds a way of expressing itself.

Panel

One form of discussion is the panel, in which from three to six people informally discuss some subject with one another under the guidance of a moderator or panel leader who introduces the subject and helps keep the discussion on the track.

The panel may be several members of a group, who meet outside to work on a special subject for presentation to the whole group. They may work alone or with the group leader. The panel may be a group of "experts," invited in for a specific purpose. Or it may be a combination of resource persons, and group members responsible for finding answers to certain questions that have arisen in the group. (With such combinations, a panel discussion may be called a colloquy.) And, instead of a panel, there may be just a dialogue, a conversation, between the people.

This approach is more often used with large groups, and yet is equally valid for small groups. To see three or four persons actually thinking together is a stimulating experience, and often brings new insights to other members of the group. In one situation, Bible study developed a real question in the group about the Christian's responsibility in social problems. They postponed consideration of the next Bible passage, and a representative committee planned for a panel of resource persons. (The planning was a learning experience in itself!) Issues in society and implications of Christianity opened up in an amazing way for the group.

Symposium

When several people prepare brief speeches in advance (*under* fifteen minutes) covering different phases of a subject, or presenting varying attitudes on some issue, we have a symposium instead of a panel.

A symposium may be a formal and impressive way to get a fair analysis of a subject or situation for a large group—or it may equally well be a sound plan in smaller groups for use of resource persons or for use of group members who will study through some phase of a question for presentation to the whole group.

Lecture

A lecture to "open channels of communication"? To increase participation? Strange as it may seem, yes. A speaker who can get the attention of the group at the beginning, and who can move along a clear route to a definite goal, often causes people to respond in an active mental participation which, though non-verbalized, leads to later effort. Giving needed information, stimulating interest, pulling segmented parts together into a meaningful whole —these things often need doing. When the lecture, or speech, does what is needed to further the progress of the group, it is not outmoded. And it is quite possible that a speech sometimes articulates the feeling and thinking of a group in a way that draws the members closer together.

Panel, Symposium, and Lecture Forums

Following a speech, speeches, or a panel, the group members almost invariably want an opportunity to question what has been said. In larger groups, questions may need to be written out and collected, but in a study group, what might be expected is that a general, informal discussion would develop, with everyone present free to participate. The discussion leader would need to possess the same skills here as in any form of discussion.

Listening Teams

Like buzz groups, listening teams are always to be used in connection with some other method. A group is divided into several parts, each part to listen or look at something with a specific question in mind. The team may meet after they have seen the film or listened to the talk or panel, to formulate their opinion about their assignment so that it can be presented by their spokesman; but more often individual members comment on their observations as they choose.

For example, in one group, as the leader introduced a study on Christian doctrine, he asked half the group to be able to list the chief theological issues of today, and the other half to be able to describe the way in which a person might develop his own faith. They listened to the introduction. Afterwards, he started by inquiring, "And now, what do those of you on the left here have to say about today's theological issues?" Then, "On the right. . . ?" In another group, viewing a film on the life of Paul, one team watched for characteristics of Paul as a person, another for difficulties he faced, another for his triumphs, and the fourth for the kind of influence he had on other people.

Circular Response

> The members of the group—not more than twenty and preferably fifteen—are seated in a circle. The chairman or leader proposes the question to be taken up. The discussion begins with the man or woman at his right. That person has the first opportunity to express his views. Then the person at *his* right has a chance to talk, and so on until the discussion has gone around the circle. No member of the group can speak a second time until his turn comes again.[6]

Accredited to Dr. Eduard Lindeman, the circular response idea is especially valuable when a controversial matter is being discussed, or when there has been difficulty in securing participation from members of the group.

Extreme views belligerently presented are modified by the restraints imposed. The timid person speaks more freely when he knows that it is his natural right as a member of the group. In some places where there is a Quaker influence a member may even delay speaking and invoke a moment of silence on the part of the whole group.[7]

It is suggested that a skillful leader will "visualize a common pot of experience as existing in the very center of the group and will help members to put their contributions into this pot instead of throwing remarks at each other."[8]

Research and Report

When individuals or small committees in a group follow the study sessions by further study and research outside, and then report on their findings, they are using a time-honored method that has proven its worth. This may take many forms, as of interviews, or opinion polls, or study of books and periodicals.

Three members of one group interviewed members of the Session about the church's policy concerning church membership with reference to race, three others found and studied official church pronouncements, and three others studied recent newspapers to see what churches had said or done to relieve racial tension.

Role-playing

The brief acting out of situations in which groups or individuals identify with other groups or individuals provides an opportunity for one person to understand how someone else feels. He takes on himself that person's point of view, and sees things from the "inside out," as it were. Or a group learns what another group said and did, as they try to reproduce for themselves certain experiences of that other group. Sometimes they prepare to meet future situations through role-playing.

This is not a rehearsed drama with the use of a prepared script. It is, perhaps, most effective when it is spontaneous. Though sometimes there is brief planning by participants in a role-playing scene, the planning is usually done by the group as a whole. Role-playing is at its best when it is used flexibly, as is needed, but perhaps these three points will be suggestive.

First, the group plans for (or structures) the role-playing scene. Here the situation is described and the characters are chosen and receive their instructions. A story may be given, with the end to be acted out. Several audio-visuals are produced with the express purpose of drawing a group into a problematic situation, and leaving them to work out their own solution. The group may set up an incident that would test a principle they have been discussing, or they may set up a modern parallel to a Biblical situation. When characters are chosen, care should be taken not to put unpopular persons in undesirable roles, and generally not to put people in roles of persons too much like themselves (although this may be necessary until a group becomes accustomed to role-playing). Sometimes a group instructs a person: "Be aggressive. Walk into that room and take control." Or sometimes incidents leading up to the situation are described, and the person is simply told to go in and try out his own ideas. Whichever plan is used, the actors need to know what is expected of them.

Second, the role-playing scene is enacted. This usually lasts only a few minutes, probably between two and ten. If people have really felt themselves into the roles of the persons they represent, the situation comes alive for them and for the group. Sometimes one part of the group is asked to identify with one actor, another part with another actor. Sometimes one person is asked to be the "conscience" of an actor, later to describe what might have been the real feelings and attitudes behind the spoken words. When the point has been made clear, and while interest is high, the group leader cuts the scene.

Third, the group discusses what has happened and often replays the scene. This is one of the most valuable steps. Probably the leader will first make inquiries of the participants: "What did you learn?" "How did you feel about . . . ?" "Were you successful in what you were trying to do?" Then he will ask other group members some questions: "If you were playing the part of Tom, how would you do it?" "Why did Mary react as she did, do you suppose?" (The assigned names would be used, rather than real names, to increase objectivity.) If it seems desirable, the scene may be replayed with the same actors, or with different ones. Usually a brief summary by the leader is profitable.

One group became the Council of Jerusalem. Another group studying Acts divided up into two's, with one person taking the role of Paul and the other of Peter, holding a conversation before the Council met. In a student group, effort was made to work out best ways of helping dissolve racial tension. One student said, "I *became* that Negro student. I *know* how he felt." Another group prepared to take an opinion poll in the community through role-playing. Members of a Youth Fellowship prepared for youth-to-youth evangelism as they played out scenes involving visits to unresponsive or antagonistic people; they not only got help in how to deal with people, but they learned their need to be able to say what they believed, and why. It is certainly true that new insights can be gained and new attitudes and skills acquired when role-playing is seriously and intelligently used.

Plays

A group may produce plays to be presented to larger audiences. Sometimes a member or members of a group may write a play, to be presented as a means of interpreting some subject to other groups. But more often, a study group will just read plays, and discuss them.

The "Temperate Zone" plays of the American Theatre Wing, written by Nora Stirling, are examples of plays designed to produce discussion. They are for parents, about the "climate of the home." (Available from National Association for Mental Health, 1780 Broadway, New York 19, N. Y.) Other discussion plays are available, about youth problems. Then there are the great plays which need only to be read by a group and appreciated with few remarks or in silence, because they speak for themselves.

Reading Books

Reading selected books, individually, and then discussing them, is as valuable for Christian groups as for the Great Books groups or informal adult education groups. When a person reads a book with the knowledge that he is to discuss it with others, he often gets more from it. Here again a teacher is needed who will help persons to go deeper than the obvious, and work at finding what is *really* being said. Sometimes, as with plays, books need only to be read aloud, with pauses and silences, without discussion. Through the reading of the book, members speak to one another.

Three women (a small study group!) met every two weeks to discuss a book they were reading. Their last one was Phillips, *Your God Is Too Small.* A student group, with a professor, decided to read aloud Kelly's *A Testament of Devotion.* What happened was that the study group became, for a period of time, a devotional group, because of the nature of the book they read. Reading books aloud, or listening to the growing number of tape and disc recordings, can both stimulate thinking and deepen the sense of fellowship in a group.

Use of Resource Persons and Materials

Probably because "experts" have learned to consider themselves resource persons and to act accordingly, few people today stand in awe before them, or accept what they say as the final word. This means that, when information is needed, it can be secured from qualified persons, where there is an opportunity for clarification through the give-and-take of conversation. Insights and information can then be related by group members to their own systems of thinking.

For a resource person to be used effectively, at least two things are essential: that the group shall understand how to use him (to be determined through discussion or role-playing); and that he shall know what is expected of him (a responsibility of the group leader). In college study groups where a faculty member or the minister to students participates, it is important to determine whether he should contribute to the discussion only when he is called upon as a resource person, or whether he should serve more as a co-leader. If each person understands his responsibility clearly, there will be no conflict.

It is equally important that resource materials should be used with a clear purpose in mind, and that these should not be brought in just to fill up time. If they are to be used to promote study, as the title "study group" would indicate, they should be related to the purpose of the study by some appropriate introduction, and used in some follow-through framework (buzz groups, listening teams, role-playing, etc.) which will help members of the group to be actively involved in consideration of the subject.

"Experts" can be brought to groups on tape recording. Documentary films bring a firsthand look at situations as they exist. Clear and complete visualization of Biblical or current life situations supply information and motivation. Charts and diagrams help clarify issues or developments.

When a group of young people began questioning the whole missionary enterprise of the Church, a film on Africa was used, and then a missionary was invited in to be interviewed by the group. Questions had been prepared in advance in buzz groups. One group brought in a Bible scholar to help in exegesis of certain difficult passages; commentaries had been used, but they wanted an opportunity to question interpretations.

Use of the Leadership Team

The leadership function need not be the sole property of one person. Often, when several persons work together, each assuming a different responsibility, the group moves more rapidly toward its goal. Certainly it would not be advisable to complicate life in a small group by regularly having too many jobs assigned. However, use of an observer or recorder has much to commend it; when a group is over fifteen in size, a steering committee may be helpful.

The recorder is that person who makes note of important decisions reached, new insights gained, or high lights of a discussion. He does not try to keep a full account, but since he does not participate he is free to concentrate on what needs to be recorded.

The observer, another silent partner, is not concerned with the content of the discussion, but only with the process itself—with what makes it move along productively, or what factors have impeded progress. At first, he may only note the number of times each person speaks, and then, reporting without the use of names, may say, "One person spoke fifteen times, one . . . , one not at all." This helps a group look at itself. At later sessions, he may try to classify remarks as to whether they are helps or hindrances. He makes notes of other factors that he, as an objective observer, would judge to have influenced group progress. The charts on the next pages may suggest how the observer would keep up with interaction among members of the group.

If the whole group can serve as a steering committee, thus all having a part in determining their own activities, it is well. If the group is too large, selected representatives, meeting with members of the leadership team, may reflect ideas and attitudes of the group as a whole as they assume planning responsibilities.

Sometimes the resource person is considered a part of the leadership team. When the chalkboard is used frequently, another team member may assume special responsibility for outlining and recording there, thus helping guide the discussion.

This use of persons not only spreads leadership responsibility, but helps a group look both at the content it is considering and at its ability to work together productively.

EVALUATION AND LEARNING

People or groups who stop to look directly at themselves and their progress toward a goal increase their ability to move directly toward and to achieve that goal. Dangerous when overused or misused, evaluation is nevertheless an

	Ed	Hor-tense	Joe	An-drew	Mrs. Buck	Geo.	Vir-ginia	Don	Roy	Ellen
Initiated	'''									
Clarified		'								
Elaborated	'''									
Integrated	'''									
Sought facts	''	''								
Analyzed		'								
Activated										
Encouraged	''	''								
Appreciated		'''								
Mediated	'									
Disciplined self	'									
Was group conscious										

	Ed	Hor-tense	Joe	An-drew	Mrs. Buck	Geo.	Vir-ginia	Don	Roy	Ellen
Dominated	'''									
Manipulated										
Blocked										
Belittled										
Distracted		'''								
Split hairs										
Just talked										

HOW TO EVALUATE

Completed Chart for Evaluating Individual Participation and Balance in a Discussion

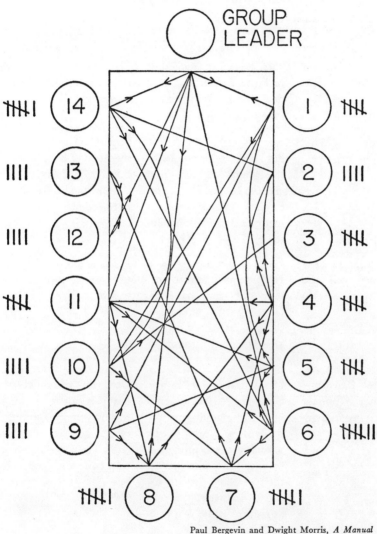

Paul Bergevin and Dwight Morris, *A Manual for Discussion Leaders and Participants.* The Seabury Press, 1954.[10]

essential element in learning. There are at least four kinds of evaluation, which may be employed at the same or at different times.

Kind of Evaluation	Values	Dangers
Purpose — "Did we achieve our purpose?"	Ties everything together in terms of purpose, and develops habit of thinking in that way.	Overuse may cause the word "purpose" to lose its meaning.
Content — "What did we learn?"	Act of verbalizing what has been learned helps the group organize and clarify its thinking, and have a sense of achievement that something actually *has* been learned.	Superficial or trite statements may be a waste of time. May force verbalizations when words are not needed.
Group Process — "How well did we work together?"	Helps all members of a group to assume responsibility for what happens. Develops in members those skills necessary for greatest group productivity.	Focuses too much attention on the process as an end in itself.
Personal Growth — "What happened to us as individuals?"	Of special value in the Christian fellowship, as a means of enabling people really to be a brother one to another, accepting and helping one another in their personal growth toward maturity. Focuses attention on the real purpose behind all study in the Christian fellowship.	Used too often when a group is not ready for it, this may cause a group to rebel. Misuse may increase introspective concern over self, or develop into competitive testimonials.

In addition to the unclassified kind of evaluation that will be going on continually in the mind of the leader, there are many ways in which evaluation may be carried out. Four suggestions are offered here.

1. *Group discussion*—either general discussion in which the leader, as a free person able and willing to accept suggestions, can establish a climate in which people can say what they really think; or buzz groups.

2. *Post-meeting reaction sheets* — to be handed in unsigned at the end of a session or unit. These may be worked out in detail by a committee of the group, or may be simple guides with such questions as these:

> What was our purpose as you saw it? ....
>
> ---
>
> Did we achieve the purpose? ..... Why or why not? ....
>
> ---

> Another grouping of questions might be this:

> What were the strong points of today's session? ....
>
> ---
>
> The weak points? ....
>
> ---
>
> What improvements would you suggest for the future? ....
>
> ---

3. *The use of the group observer*—who, having watched activities objectively, may be able to report in such a way that the group sees itself for the first time. He may

lead in a discussion, with questions and comments like these: "It seemed to me that we bogged down at this point. . . ." "Perhaps it was because . . . What do you think?" Or, "I wondered how Jack felt when two people started . . ."

4. *Listening to a tape recording of a session*—and evaluating it as a group.

MOTIVATION AND LEARNING

"If only we could solve the problem of motivation," educators are saying, "we could solve the problem of learning." Certainly leaders are increasingly aware of the importance of motivation, but none pretend to know all the answers. Some people feel that motivation entirely precedes learning; these would believe an inspiring talk delivered in advance might move a person, for example, to join a study group and put forth diligent effort, insuring learning. But experience would perhaps indicate that motivation is more complex than this, that it must somehow be "built in" all the processes of setting goals and making decisions and being confronted with truth through ideas and personal relationships. Original motivation needs to be strengthened through needs met and values gained from the experience; and, as a person becomes involved, as he gives himself, his motivation becomes stronger, and, in turn, he receives more. Perhaps this is another way of saying, at least for the Christian fellowship, that participation in that fellowship should in itself provide motivation for sustained effort. Might not an "outsider" in this way become a Christian?

The ideal, of course, would be that each group member might be the kind of person who, committed to the Christian cause, would be able to see purposes clearly and give himself to them, making them his own. Because he would be capable of seeing and responding to the intrinsic value of the truth he studied, concern over trivialities would be at a minimum. But if even a few people like this are present in a group, the group has its beginning point. Petty concerns and lower motives may be replaced by higher, more comprehensive ones, as a group exerts its influence over its members.

PLANNING A STUDY SESSION

When a leader can state in one sentence what the purpose of a session is; when all that he knows about motivation and subject matter and methods are no longer unrelated facts but interwoven parts of one whole; when methods combine and re-combine and can be used without names; when members of the group live and move before the leader—then everything falls into place, and the leader is ready for the session. It is there before him; he sees it, complete.

Yet he knows that the tentative outline which he has formulated with care will probably be changed as he responds to the group. That outline will help the leader have enough confidence to begin—and to change. It will include at least these parts:

Purpose.

An idea for getting started.

Some questions or a plan for getting into the subject fully.

An idea for concluding.

Any leader will have to work out his own best approach to preparation for a session, remembering that unless he prepares, unless he can see and feel the vitality of the ideas and facts being studied, it is not likely that other members will succeed where he has failed. And his own spiritual preparation not only precedes but is concurrent with his preparation to lead the group in study.

We Study the Bible

Not because what has been said is irrelevant to study of the Bible, but rather because of the primary importance of the Bible to the Church, a brief look directly at this one area of study should prove helpful.

THE BIBLE IN THE CHRISTIAN FELLOWSHIP

The Church today and her mission in the world may be understood only in the light of her heritage, preserved and made available through the Bible. We who are Christians are identified with and actors in the same drama as that early community of chosen persons. Bound together with them by a common loyalty to the eternal God, our history is but a continuation of theirs—the story of God's dealings with man. No part can be understood apart from its relationship to the whole story. This is one reason why the Bible is and always must be at the heart of study within the Christian fellowship.

There is another reason. Through the Bible God speaks to us. Alan Richardson expresses

> the deep conviction that the Bible is the covenanted means of God's self-communication with men, and that because God has appointed it for this purpose it possesses a value which no other book could ever have.[1]

Opening ourselves to receive the revelation of Himself that God has made available, we find that the Bible contains for us, too, the Word of God—and that it confronts us with the ultimate revelation, Jesus Christ, the "Word made flesh." It is therefore true that the Bible *does* something to us, as well as *says* something to us. ". . . these are written that you may believe that Jesus is the Christ, the Son of God, and that believing you may have life in his name." (John 20:31, R.S.V.)

This is not to suggest that *only* the Bible is the proper study for Christians. In this complex world we need all the help we can muster from one another to see the Christian answers to the issues that face us. What Suzanne de Dietrich finds true for college students is true for other groups as well.

> . . . for students Bible study is starved unless it is accompanied by serious study of a non-biblical kind. . . . We are inhabitants of a complex world, and in a democratic society each of us has to decide about questions which demand the mastery of facts and the cultivation of sound judgment, for which habits of devotion by themselves can never be a substitute.[2]

Nansie Blackie, speaking again of college students, says,

Apart from Bible study, it is likely that subjects covered will fall under four very general headings: doctrine, social and political questions, problems of "personal" life, and specific university concerns.[3]

THE UNIQUENESS OF BIBLE STUDY

There are many ways in which all study is alike, whether it be of the Bible or of something else. The humility to admit he does not know all the answers, the discipline and the honesty to follow after truth wherever it may lead— these qualities any student needs. All that has been said about purpose, involvement, interpersonal relationships, motivation, and evaluation, is relevant. Because method is always to be chosen in terms of content and purpose, what has been said about method is pertinent. That is, any methods suggested here, *appropriately chosen,* would be usable in Bible study. As a matter of fact, judging from what Bernhard Anderson says, the best known methods of research and the most effective procedures for achieving emotional identification are required.

If we are to hear God's Word spoken through the Bible to our situation today, our first task is to put ourselves within the world of the Bible. No casual or superficial reading of Scripture can accomplish this. We must avail ourselves of the results of historical criticism and biblical theology so that we may imaginatively relive the actual historical situation in which an Amos or a Paul heard the high calling of God. We must, as it were, sit where these ancient people sat and learn to look at the human scene from their unique point of view. We must live with the Bible until it becomes part of us, just as the actor identifies himself with the role that he plays. It is then, perhaps, that the Holy Spirit, breathing through the ancient words of the sacred page, will lead us to know that the "Word of the Lord" spoken by the prophets and embodied in Jesus Christ is actually the deepest interpretation of our own life situation and our world crisis in the twentieth century.[4]

The uniqueness of Bible study lies, not in the methods used, but in that which is studied—the Bible itself—and in one's attitude toward it.

Content *in itself,* important as methods are, says something. When people come to understand what the Bible is saying, they are confronted with God and His self-revelation.

> One may come to the Bible for all kinds of reasons . . . But when we launch on such a search we soon find that roles are interchanged; instead of questioning, we are questioned; we wanted to form a personal judgment about the Bible; we were attending a trial and here we are sitting on the bench of the accused. The Bible comes to us with searching questions, which it becomes increasingly difficult to avoid if we want to be quite honest; difficult to avoid because they strike right at the heart of our being. Modern theological language calls these questions "existential" because they become a matter of life and death to those concerned as soon as they take them seriously.[5]

It soon becomes apparent that all the time God was there, taking the initiative in seeking man. Man does not "discover" God. His part is to listen and respond. Miss de Dietrich says that all the questions asked of man through the Bible come down to one, the one with which God sought Adam when he ran away to hide in the Garden of Eden: "Where are you?"

"Where are you?" The Bible really speaks to us when this question comes to us as the question that we are bound to answer and when we allow ourselves to be searched and questioned. Then and then only does the Bible unfold before our dazzled eyes the abundance of God's forgiveness and mercy, of God's searching love and redeeming power. Then He comes to us as Lord and Saviour in this person-to-person encounter which changes the whole meaning of a man's life.[6]

Note the statement, "when we allow ourselves to be searched and questioned." This suggests the second point of that which makes for uniqueness in Bible study—the attitude with which one approaches such a study. This openness, this receptivity, is necessary if Bible study is to achieve its purpose. It involves a reverence, a willingness to accept the authority of the Bible, and a knowledge that an act of the will is the inevitable outcome when insights come home to a person.

. . . the Bible tells us very clearly that to "know" God is not an affair of the mind only, but an act in which our whole being, heart, mind, and will, is vitally engaged; so that sheer intellectual speculation would enable us to form certain ideas about God but never to "know" Him. To be grasped God's will must be met with a readiness to obey.[7]

But this does not give to any one person the right to say that he, and he alone, has the correct interpretation of the Bible. To do this would give to the one person the authority rightly belonging to the Bible. If that person, in the light of the Church's historical understanding of what the Bible means, would approach the study reverently, *along with others,* the group would not go astray.

Nor does this mean that any person has the right to sit in judgment on any other person, or that the skeptic cannot help sharpen perception of truth for a believer, or that original less worthy attitudes and motives cannot be transformed to become those which are needed for fruitful Bible study.

SUGGESTIONS ABOUT PROCEDURE

Experiences of Bible study groups in many countries, especially of college student groups, increasing rapidly since World War II, have brought forth some helpful practical suggestions.

Beginning either with a period of prayer* or of silence, sometimes a silence in which members re-read the passage for the day, which they have previously studied and on which they have meditated, the leader may give a brief introduction or offer such background information as is needed. Or a group member may introduce the subject, with all members doing this in turn. Miss de Dietrich suggests that the introduction should not last more than ten minutes, and "should remain close to the text and raise well-pointed questions for discussion."[8]

As the group moves into the discussion, different procedures are possible. Bernhard Anderson suggests this:

... you may decide to ask someone to read the passage, or

---

* Note this comment from "Study Groups and Their Leadership," p. 23:

One question to be faced at the start will be whether the group should begin with prayer. If non-Christians are present, prayer may be such as to involve an assent to the Christian faith which they are not yet prepared to give. In such a case a period of reverent silence might be held: or a prayer that the members might be led to the truth might be quite in place.

a small unit of it, aloud. If there are difficult words, they should be explained. Perhaps light from another translation should be sought.

Sometimes groups have found it helpful to begin the discussion by attempting to paraphrase the passage in modern language, that is, "put it in your own words." This is a good discipline, for it demands (1) coming to terms with what the original writer meant to say, and (2) attempting to translate that meaning into our own categories. This may occasion the interaction between the world of the Bible and our world, which is the very essence of Bible conversation.[9]

Throughout the discussion, Dr. Anderson advises, the group should not be afraid of "unorthodox" questions (note earlier comments on "brainstorming"). "On the other hand," he adds, "don't be afraid of 'orthodoxy'— only try to 'beat the crust back into the batter' of Christian experience."[10]

Sometimes groups use questionnaires as discussion aids; at times the introduction is omitted, and the questionnaire serves as a guide for the whole discussion. The leader must take care to have questions lead back to the text, if he is to avoid the danger of which Miss de Dietrich warns, that this method may lead to "exegesis of the questionnaire rather than of the Bible text itself."[11] If it is to be used, she says, the questionnaire should be prepared by students, who follow certain principles both in their private study and in their preparation of the questions.

How to study a passage and prepare a questionnaire [12]

(The following rules are not absolute nor to be taken as such, but they have proved of some use on many occasions.)

When we study a given passage we should take the following steps:

(a) Look for the relation of the passage to its context.

(b) Look for its meaning in its historical and general setting.

(c) Translate it into terms of ordinary speech and find its central point.

(d) Place it in the context of the Christian message as a whole.

What specific message is it meant to convey?

(e) Look for the important and difficult words (difficult because we do not understand them or because we have heard them so often that they have lost their meaning for us!).

What is their contemporary meaning?

(f) Note the relevance of the passage for us personally, and as a Church.

How does it affect what we believe and what we do?

. . . Our first question will bear on the main meaning of the passage studied. What is it meant to convey? We shall then take up the main verses, or words, one by one: what do they mean? We shall refer to parallel verses . . . we shall ask some questions pointing to the relevance of this passage to our own situation.

A good question is a question which forces us back to the text studied and constrains us to dig deeper into its meaning. The best way to test a questionnaire is to try to answer it ourselves; we then see that certain questions are bad because the answer is too self-evident, others because there is no definite answer, the question being either too involved or too vague. Practical applications to the present situation should only be entered into when the meaning of the passage has been made quite clear.

It should be obvious that "questionnaire," as used here, refers not to a multiple-choice objective check-list, but to a series of questions designed to provoke thought and to serve as a discussion guide.

Help in private study, or in preparation of questions for group discussion, might be found in Dr. J. M. Gettys' suggestions[13] about approaching study through analysis of paragraphs as to key persons, places, events, and ideas, and his plan for finding the relationship of ideas.

The pattern of the discussion may depend more on the leader's personal preparation, as he takes the initiative in moving the group on to another block of Scripture, or unit of thought, as he senses their readiness to proceed.

Because Bible study is found in both conferences and retreats, these two ideas are offered by Miss de Dietrich:

(a) the lecture on the passage by an expert comes first and the assembly splits into small groups for discussion;

(b) the topic is first studied within the small groups and this is a kind of joint preparation for the lecture and general discussion which follows. This second method has sometimes proved most fruitful. It can be applied also in the life of the local group; the members meet one week in small groups by themselves, and the following week with the competent leader who lectures on the subject and answers questions.[14]

Whatever the procedure pattern, leaders of Bible study groups seem generally agreed on two major questions that must be kept in mind; in some way or ways, these questions need to be considered, the first before the second.

First, *what is this passage saying?* This means giving people an opportunity to say what it seems to them to be saying. It means checking the text, and translations, and commentaries for needed information about historical and cultural background and explanation of terms. It means, as has been said, finding "Who is saying what to whom in what circumstances?"[15] Before we can know what the passage is really saying, it must be interpreted in the light of the whole Bible revelation. So the group struggles to determine exactly what the message is. Then, and only then, does the second question open.

Second, *what does this message say to us, today?* This involves both self-knowledge and knowledge of many areas, and is difficult for both group and individual. It is the part which leads to change. But there is no easy "application" to be superimposed upon life today. As Bernhard Anderson says,

> Remember that "the letter killeth; it is the Spirit that giveth Life." The Bible should not be treated as a soothsayer's manual which gives us literal, specific directives on everything under the sun. As John Casteel has said, there are some places in the Bible where God does not say anything to us except, perhaps, "go read a commentary."[16]

Including the same questions but interpreted in terms of *movement toward relevance* is a plan, "Depth Bible Study," developed and used experimentally by William P. Anderson, Jr., with many adult groups. He describes the plan as follows:

> The process begins in phase 1 when, after members of the group have read independently of each other a passage of Scripture, they meet together to identify what they as a group believe that the passage means. In this, there is, of course, movement from individual positions to a group position.

Then after the group has identified its conclusions, the thoughts of commentators and Biblical students are thrown into the discussion so that the group may then move from its original to some new position if that seems desirable. Thus a second movement has taken place.

Then for the third step, the leader of the group seeks to help the group find what the implications of the Scripture passage are for living relationships in which members of the group find themselves. In this third step, it would seem to me reasonable to believe that still further movement takes place as the group is face to face with God's will in relation to their own lives. Obviously, some members of the group when thus confronted may choose to refuse to do the will of God, but I believe that facing the will of God in a Christian group in this way can prove to be a strong encouragement toward movement to accept and do His will. In this way, the Gospel can become relevant to every man who studies it.[17]

A teacher of an adult Sunday school class, in using this plan, has these comments to make:

As this lesson progressed, the teacher realized that something was taking place in the class that had not taken place before. The members were applying the lesson to themselves. Three weeks ago the experiment was equally successful with the intensive study of the Golden Rule in the 6th chapter. One of the members raised what he said was a personal problem with him: should he lend money to a friend who wanted to go into business; another raised the question of giving to someone whom you know to be an alcoholic. . . . When the discussion was over, most of us felt shaken up and much less complacent about the Golden Rule than we had before.[18]

This teacher recognizes some dangers.

Our natural reaction is always to apply the judgment in the Scripture to someone else. . . . Another danger is that the answers come too glibly and you end up with a collection of platitudes. . . . Another difficulty is the natural tendency to bog down in abstract problems of theology or criticism.[19]

A good leader and a responsible group will learn how to avoid these dangers. They will learn how to use varied and appropriate methods during the different steps of the study—as, for example, the use of a resource person (or, better, of a group member appointed to be the resource person for the session) in phase two.

These procedures have proved profitable, but there is need for experimentation with other procedures, and for diligent effort to understand the Bible message, and to take that message seriously.

Group Study and the Christian Fellowship

From the Section on Evangelism of the Evanston Conference comes a statement which, in essence, summarizes the reasons for the emphasis here given to the importance of and need for group study in the Christian fellowship.

> The Church which God uses to communicate the gospel is a fellowship, a *koinonia,* drawn and held together by the love of Christ through the power of the Holy Spirit and by the need and desire of its members to share this experience with each other and to draw those outside into that *koinonia.* The evangelizing Church will offer this gift in its preaching and teaching; in its acts of worship and administration of its sacraments; through the individual and group witness of its members; by leading its people to base their life upon God's Word used in personal and family devotions; by fostering small fellowships; and by works of social service.[1]

Since this fellowship enters a group and becomes a growing reality only through the presence of persons who have themselves experienced the transforming love of Christ— a small minority, perhaps, but a redemptive one—it is necessary to look at the opportunities and responsibilities of those persons, both leaders and group members, through whom the gospel is to be communicated. And since one of the tasks of the church, wherever located, is to plan for "small fellowships," it should be helpful to give some consideration to preparation for them within the framework of the total program.

THE LEADER

Perhaps Ruth Brown had thought of herself as a dynamic person who could "manage" a group with ease, and she had failed to live up to her own self-expectations. Or perhaps she had counted more on her personality than on preparation, more on the prestige of the leader's role than on a mastery of subject matter and a genuine quality of leadership. At any rate, she left the first meeting of the new group at the church with a defeated feeling. Some comments from three members of the group as they drove home throw further light on the subject: "I thought at first it was going to be wonderful. Ruth just sparkled, didn't she? But *something* happened. I think she was unhappy with us when we didn't enter the discussion. You know, when she'd finished talking, she said, 'Are there any questions?' and then kept on with, 'I want you to feel perfectly free to say what's on your mind. Everybody should enter into the discussion.' I couldn't think of a question to ask or a comment to make to save my life!" The second person said, "Nor I. I was never sure what we were to discuss—or, for that matter, why we were meeting." The third person concluded, "Well, we've got to *act* interested next time, anyway. I got the feeling Ruth was worried about what we thought of her as a leader."

It happens all too frequently that a leader tells people to participate instead of creating a situation in which they *can participate*—in which, sometimes, they are surprised to discover how vitally involved they are. Or a leader is more concerned with what people think of *him* than he is with what is really happening to *them*. Actually, when a group has had one of its best sessions, members may be entirely unaware of the leader as a person, or of his part in the picture.

To be a leader is not an easy thing. What is demanded is not a "glorious" leader who draws those lesser persons who are his followers to him in a personal devotion which may obscure the real purpose of the group. A dictator would never be willing to let people become themselves, any more than he would know how to help them in that process. The laissez-faire person who proudly announces that he has little to do because he believes in "permissive" leadership usually finds that the group ends up as a chaotic collection of confused individuals. Rather, the leader who is needed is a redeemed Christian, willing to make all the resources of his life available to the group, whom he sees as persons of worth and dignity in their own right.

Because this person is a Christian, his motives are not self-seeking. He sees himself as the servant of the group, not its master. He is willing to accept criticism, to absorb hostility, even to fail and try again. Because his is the ministry of reconciliation, he so identifies himself with those in the group that he suffers and rejoices with and for them. His prayers for them, his visits and calls, arise from the concept of the ministry that is his.

When these things are true, the leader listens to people —*really* listens—because he believes they have something to say, and because he sees them as *persons*. Perhaps because he *expects* something from them and *believes* in them an atmosphere is created which actually helps them contribute. He respects people enough not to intrude upon their privacy nor to force them to verbalize ideas before they are ready nor to try to change them to fit some mold he has in mind. These attitudes, toward himself and toward those in the group, express themselves in the tone of his voice, in the suggestions he makes to the group as to how they might move purposefully toward a goal, and in all the intangible areas of interpersonal relationships.

So it is that he tries to master the skills of the group process, not in order that he might manipulate the group to his own ends, thus experiencing a feeling of power, but in order that he might help people communicate with one another. He tries to learn to become whatever the group needs him to be.

The techniques at his disposal in addition to his own relationship, which is non-verbal, are question-making, restatement, or articulation of their formulation, interpretation of situations, the making of suggestions, and the giving of information when such is relevant. He stands neither on top of the group as a dictator nor outside the group as an objective observer, but takes his place within the group as participant-interpreter. He is a catalyst, a gadfly, a guide, a friend, and a fund of useful information. Occasionally he is an anchor, an interpreter, or an immovable object.[2]

To some people this kind of flexibility, this free use of methods that draw people into the group and help them communicate, this ease and warmth and understanding, seem as natural as breathing. When this is so, it is not because they have memorized the characteristics of a good leader and mastered them like rules of grammar, but because their way of working is a consistent expression of what they believe and are.

And it is true, for this kind of Christian leader, that when something real happens in a group—when a person gains a new perspective or shows courage in a decision or utters a few revealing words in a prayer at the end of a session—he knows this is not of his doing, but that he has witnessed the miracle of God at work with man, seeking him in love and confronting him with the call to discipleship.

THE GROUP MEMBER

There are not too many differences in the leader and in other group members. It is a costly thing to be the kind of leader that has been described; similarly, any group member who sees what the group is really for gives up forever the luxury of being a spectator, sitting passively to have something done to or for him. Instead, he takes upon himself the work of being a ministering servant and a responsible participant. His calling to the "ministry of the laity" means that there are things he will need to do for and with individuals outside the study sessions. There are many times, in these days, when Christians need one another, just as there are times when others need to have communicated to them, in act and in word, the reality of Christian love.

Sometimes groups progress to the point of making leadership a consciously shared function. There may be coleaders, there may be a rotating leadership, or some other plan may be used. Certainly it is true in the kind of group that has been envisioned here that the burden of the success or failure of the group does not rest on one person. Franklyn Haiman says, as do others, that a good leader should try to work himself out of the leader's role. He believes that members of the group should take upon themselves more and more of the leadership functions that are needed.

> To the degree, for example, that each of the members of the group develops the ability to be more objective in discussing conflicts of opinion, the leader becomes free to cast off his cloak of super-human impartiality and gains the right to have a subjective view. To the degree that each of the members disciplines his own contributions, learning to stick to the point and letting others be heard, the leader can throw away his policeman's badge. To the degree that each of the members exerts some initiative in stimulating personal involvement or provoking hard thinking in the group, the leader need no longer strain himself to be a scintillating dynamo of intellectual genius and social skills. He can become what he really is—a human being.[3]

One group, in a whole evening given to evaluation, decided to work out a self check-list, to be used by all group members as they endeavored to become the best possible kind of participant. Such a list might include the following questions:

1. Did I prepare before I came, both by prayer and study?

2. Did I really try to listen to every person and understand exactly what he was saying?

3. Did I monopolize conversation? Or, when I spoke, did I have something relevant to contribute, or a question to ask that helped us move along in our thinking?

4. Did I make any effort to help when I saw something was needed—either a question or a fact or a response to some person? Or did I just feel critical and do nothing?

5. Was I honest? Or did I say what I thought the group expected?

6. Did I make an effort to think and speak clearly, and to listen to others expectantly, believing that God can and does speak through us to one another?

7. Am I willing to follow through on implications for myself of any truth I glimpsed? Or do I see only what it means for someone else?

Learning how to be a good member does not mean

learning how to fit a pattern, nor losing oneself in a group. Nothing could be more boring and unproductive than for every person in a group to be just alike. Nor would it be interesting to be a part of a group where all were too polite, or overly concerned to the point of sentimentality, or non-committal. This is not what is meant by interest in and respect for one another. Persons of integrity—and every group member, including the leader, has not only the right but the responsibility to maintain his own inner integrity—are needed if a group is to be vital. Different personalities with the unique gifts of each enrich a group.

That person who has experienced the reality of the doctrine of the "priesthood of believers" knows what it really means to be a member of a Christian group.

> God does not leave any of us to stand alone. In every place He has gathered us together to be His family, in which His gifts and His forgiveness are received. Do you forgive one another as Christ forgave you? Is your congregation a true family of God, where every man can find a home and know that God loves him without limit?[4]

PLANNING FOR STUDY GROUPS

Before the values of group study for the Christian fellowship can be realized in the life of that fellowship, specific planning must be done by responsible churchmen who study the implications for them of such fundamental assumptions and suggestions as have been offered here. There are several areas about which they will be concerned in their planning.

About the Relation of Study to Other
Aspects of the Program

While group study is a teaching, evangelizing tool of
the church, within which members may find mental and
spiritual health, it is but one aspect of the life of the
church, of her worship and service. It is an integral part
of that life, influencing and being influenced by what goes
on elsewhere in the fellowship. Any group responsible for
over-all planning must always be able to see and plan for
the balance and interaction of the parts.

Even within a study group, study is not the only element. The genuine fellowship that develops means that
people have experiences of worship together. Sometimes
they agree to pray for one another, or to adopt certain
disciplines of personal devotional life which will be more
meaningful because they are shared by others. This illus-
trates the fact that one experience of life cannot be com-
partmentalized from another, because a person is an or-
ganic whole. A person does not study one day, worship the
next day within a designated fifteen-minute time, and
have "fellowship" in a brief social period where almost
complete strangers rush through the act of drinking a cup
of coffee. Rather, when group members are willing to
spend time with one another, they will profit from relax-
ing and having fun together—and the fun, in turn, deep-
ens the fellowship. These occasional social meetings have
a valid place in the life of a study group. Moreover, study
may lead into action.[5] Seeing clearly what something says
to them, a group may be moved to undertake some group

action; this motivation ought to lead to opportunities for action, and not always to frustration (as is so often the case). Later, the group would return to more intensive study.

When a group becomes a working, worshiping, studying group, then fellowship becomes a reality, and life is viewed as a whole. Sometimes a retreat, lasting several days, where people live together, and worship and study together, can provide a kind of intensive experience which will be invaluable in the development of the life of the group.

Of course it sometimes happens that a group becomes an entity within itself, and somehow loses contact with other groups, or with the church. An adult Sunday school class can become a miniature church, a law unto itself; a group of college students can become a clique. Actually, the small group, where there is an intimate, face-to-face fellowship, is only a channel for finding one's place in that great, ongoing company of persons who constitute the Church.

About Setting Up the Groups

For the college campus, several approaches have been suggested for the structure of the study aspect of the Westminster Fellowship (the Presbyterian, U.S., program for the college campus).

Possible approaches:

A. As a structural part of the Westminster Fellowship
   —as part of the Program Commission and thus related to program.

—or under a Vice-President in charge of study groups, and thus tied in with the Council.

—under a "Study Secretary" who sets up groups, obtains materials, reminds members at first, etc.

Can be set up:

a) on a graded basis with flexibility in selection of specific directions . . . [The Princeton plan does this by providing opportunities for study in four areas, The Student and the Church, The Student and the Bible, The Student and World Struggle, and The Student, the University, and Culture, for each of the four college years.]

b) before the semester begins, on the basis of previous interest worked out in the spring and set up during the summer.

c) after school begins, on the basis of interest indicated by new students, choosing from an inclusive list.

d) spontaneously throughout the school year, upon the request of students and indication of sufficient interest; following a particular program or series on Sunday evening, or about some particular problem which arises (e.g. desegregation, academic freedom, unionization, etc.).

B. As a particular and limited program emphasis . . .

. . . a series of simultaneous studies done over a particular period: e.g. Lenten study groups.

Hazen suppers in the spring at U. of Texas.

Home seminar programs with faculty at Yale . . .

Membership study groups, YMCA-UNC, '47.

C. As part of other aspects of the program . . .

. . . occasional study retreats or study periods on regular retreats.

... study in Cabinet or Council meetings, at the first of each meeting (not less than 30 minutes!) or every other meeting for entire time.[6]

In local churches, the Christian Education Committee, the Church Planning Committee, and the Session, planning with the individuals and groups involved, may take all or any one of the three steps suggested here.

1. Encourage existing groups to make use of relevant ideas about group study. Sunday school classes, leadership education classes, circles, small study groups that have sprung up spontaneously—such groups may wish to continue with their organizational pattern but work more on ways of studying together.

2. Modify conditions, where this is needed, to make more effective study possible. For example, what can be done about time, and about the size of groups? Miss de Dietrich recommends an hour's time for most groups, stating forty-five minutes as a real minimum.[7] She recommends about eight to ten as the best number for a group. Is there some way smaller Sunday school classes for adults could be set up? Or could large classes be divided into smaller study groups, coming together occasionally for information from the teacher (who meets between times with group leaders) and for exchange of ideas? The need for regular and prepared participation will be met as members have the idea behind group study interpreted to them, and as they become involved in it.

3. Plan to meet needs not now being met by setting up new groups and exploring the possibilities of revising certain parts of the program. Some of the cells and other groups that have sprung up spontaneously, some of the experiences of study groups on the college campus, have suggested new possibilities to the local church. There is nothing sacred about the man-made Sunday school schedule, for example; some groups might be able to study together better at another time. Paul Maves points out the need for churches to experiment in the area of setting up groups where they can mean most to people.

> . . . every person who seeks membership in the Church will be related to a small, intimate, face-to-face group which will meet frequently over a period of time and in the spirit of *agape* for fellowship, study, worship, and service. This may mean that the large congregation will have to be sub-divided into classes, societies, zones, cell groups, and recreational groups.[8]

He says that these groups will not be set up on "the basis of convenient statistical categories," and the size of groups will not be determined "by publicity values." Rather, there will be groupings according to interests, such as young parents, engaged couples, etc., and "consideration will be given to the possibilities of working with natural and primary groups in the community."

> Such groups as families, neighborhood groups, gangs, and social sets, as well as professional and work groups may be approached and perhaps incorporated into the

Christian community. Cottage prayer meetings, neighbor-hood church-school classes, block organizations, and a fam-ily-centered program are examples of possible approaches to this.[9]

The Evanston Report speaks of the need for the Church to "come to life in small neighborhoods," and points to the emergence of the Christian community "whose locus is the factory, the mine, the office, the waterfront, the university."[10]

About Materials

What is to be studied? In college student groups, the materials suggested here have been used.

Possible bases for study:

—a single book — should be available in inexpensive edition for all to purchase, concise and consistent presentation. (e.g. Niles' *That They May Have Life,* Whale's *Christian Doctrine,* Tillich's *Shaking of the Foundations,* etc.)

—a study book — preferably prepared for students and draw-ing upon available references and resources. (e.g., USCC's *The Christian Student in the University,* NSCY's *Where Are You?, Your Freedom Is in Trouble,* etc.)

—an outline — drawing upon various books and sources, pre-pared beforehand to fit the needs and interests of the par-ticular group . . .

—an outline — developed from week to week guided by previ-ous discussion and interest and presented each week as the basis for that discussion . . .

—a series of books. . . .[11]

In local churches, the regular printed curriculum helps may continue to be used. Books of the Bible, along with commentaries and other aids to interpretation, may be selected. Study courses may be chosen on the basis of interest finders. Books and periodicals may be used.

As plans progress, at least two principles should be remembered: (1) that the people who are to do the studying need to be involved in the planning of *what* they will study; and (2) that some balanced and intelligent plan should be worked out by the group members involved and the official church planning committee, probably the Christian Education Committee. The long-range implications of what is being done must be considered. One group called "The Newcomers," for example, planning to go through the Bible book by book, discovered a weakness in this plan.

> This approach lasted through seven books of the Old Testament and two teachers. By this time certain limitations of the method became apparent. It became questionable whether the class members would live long enough ever to reach the New Testament. Certainly they would no longer be Newcomers when they did so.[12]

Moreover, in keeping with the statement that a "good curriculum possesses the qualities of comprehensiveness, balance, and sequence,"[13] groups should be encouraged to avoid any haphazard approach to choice of study material. High school youth, for instance, *might* thoughtlessly and irresponsibly choose to study "boy-girl relationships" month in and month out. This is an extreme, of course, but suggests the need, from time to time, to consider what we *should* know and not just the interest of the moment.

As groups develop the habit of thoughtful planning, and of watching decisions to determine their implications, and as they reach the point of studying and working together freely, it is easy to imagine that, beginning with some basic study, they might go off on by-paths as needed, and then return. In a study of Paul's Epistles, for example, they might become involved in some current issues, stop for a study there, return and continue. Or they might stop to study *The Confession of Faith*. This, however, is more in the area of possibility than of tested experience. It needs experimentation.

About Methods in General

The eager-eyed young teacher who rushes up to inquire breathlessly, "How can I get my pupils to participate?" cannot be answered with a list of methods. Rather, the answer is a question: "How do you feel about people? Do you believe in them, respect them, care for them?" The experienced lecturer who says, "But I must tell them about the gospel message; I must be sure they get to the heart of the matter . . ." must also be answered with a question: "And when *is* the gospel actually communicated? Is it not true that the act of revelation is completed with the act of response, and thus becomes communication?" Those leaders who work with people in study groups must constantly recall that methods are expressions of attitudes and convictions, that they spring from what we believe about people and about the way in which persons are born into the Christian faith, and grow toward maturity.

The same things are true for planning groups. Arbitrary plans superimposed upon people who are then encouraged to "participate" are to be questioned. Methods there, too, are ways of making real that quality of life characteristic of the Christian fellowship.

About Leadership Education

This suggestion is offered about leader preparation in student groups:

> ... leaders should have:
>> a retreat for leadership training and preparatory study.
>> a regular time for meeting with the Minister to Students for progress reporting, suggestions, and help.
>> a monthly meeting with other leaders for sharing of insights and problems.[14]

For any group, all the tested methods of leader development, in leadership education classes, through observation and apprenticeship, and in other ways, are valuable. However, learning to be a responsible group participant is the first step for the group leader. The experience of being a part of a functioning group will help produce leaders because it will help with motivation at the same time it offers an opportunity to develop needed skills. A concept of leadership that no longer makes everything dependent on the leader will help. In the final analysis, small fellowships may be able to produce their own leaders.

And it is to be remembered that the Christian leader who has himself been confronted by Jesus Christ does not become one who does something to other people, tries to make something happen to them, while he himself remains untouched. Rather, he continues to learn, with others, and to open himself to the healing, transforming power of the fellowship of which he is a part.

For Further Reading

Working With Groups

Anderson, Frances M., *Team Teaching in Christian Education.* Chicago: Evangelical Covenant Church of America, 1967.

Anderson, Philip A., *Church Meetings That Matter.* Boston: United Church Press, 1965.

Bowman, Locke E., *Straight Talk About Teaching in Today's Church.* Philadelphia: The Westminster Press, 1967.

Case, Lambert J., *How to Reach Group Decisions.* St. Louis: Bethany Press, 1958.

Casteel, John (ed.), *Spiritual Renewal Through Personal Groups.* New York: Association Press, 1957.

Douglass, Paul F., *The Group Workshop Way in the Church.* New York: Association Press, 1956.

Douty, Mary Alice, *How to Work with Church Groups.* Nashville: Abingdon Press, 1957.

Gable, Lee J. (ed.), *Encyclopedia for Church Group Leaders.* New York: Association Press, 1959.

Gilbert, W. Kent, *As Christians Teach.* Philadelphia: Fortress Press, 1962.

Haiman, Franklyn S., *Group Leadership and Democratic Action.* New York: Houghton Mifflin, 1951.

Hill, Doris J., *Teaching: the inside story.* Philadelphia: Board of Christian Education, United Presbyterian Church U.S.A., 1967.

Howe, Reuel L., *The Miracle of Dialogue.* Greenwich, Conn.: Seabury Press, 1963.

Klein, Alan F., *How to Use Role Playing Effectively.* New York: Association Press, 1959.

Kuhn, Margaret E., *You Can't Be Human Alone*. New York: National Council of the Churches, 1956.

Leypeldt, Martha M., *40 Ways to Teach in Groups*. Valley Forge: Judson Press, 1967.

McKinley, John, *Creative Methods for Adult Classes*. St. Louis: Bethany Press, 1960.

Miles, Matthew B., *Learning to Work in Groups*. New York: Bureau of Publications, Teachers College, Columbia University, 1959.

Bible Study

Anderson, Bernhard W., *Rediscovering the Bible*. New York: Association Press, 1951.

Anderson, Bernhard W., *The Unfolding Drama of the Bible*. New York: Association Press, 1953.

Concise Concordance to the Revised Standard Version of the Holy Bible. New York: Thomas Nelson & Sons, 1959.

Cully, Iris V., *Imparting the Word: The Bible in Christian Education*. Philadelphia: The Westminster Press, 1963.

de Dietrich, Suzanne, *God's Unfolding Purpose: A Guide to the Study of the Bible*. Philadelphia: The Westminster Press, 1960.

Denbeaux, Fred J., *Understanding the Bible*. Philadelphia: The Westminster Press, 1958.

Dodd, C. H., *The Bible Today*. London and New York: Cambridge University Press, 1946.

Dummelow, J. R. (ed.), *The One Volume Bible Commentary*. New York: Macmillan, 1936, 1955.

Gettys, Joseph M., *How to Enjoy Studying the Bible*. Richmond: John Knox Press, revised, 1946. Enlarged edition, 1956.

Gettys, Joseph M., *How to Teach the Bible*. Richmond: John Knox Press, revised, 1961.

Harkness, Georgia, *Toward Understanding the Bible*. New York: Abingdon-Cokesbury, 1952.

Jones, Clifford M., *The Bible Today: For Those Who Teach It.* Philadelphia: Fortress Press, 1964.

Kelly, Balmer H. (ed.), *Introduction to the Bible* (Volume 1, Layman's Bible Commentary). Richmond: John Knox Press, 1959.

Koenig, Robert E., *The Use of the Bible with Adults.* Philadelphia: The Christian Education Press, 1959.

Richardson, Alan, *A Preface to Bible Study.* Philadelphia: The Westminster Press, 1944.

Robertson, E. H., *Take and Read: A Guide to Group Bible Study.* Richmond: John Knox Press, 1961.

Rolston, Holmes, *The Bible in Christian Teaching.* Richmond: John Knox Press, 1962.

Westminster Dictionary of the Bible. Philadelphia: The Westminster Press, 1944.

Westminster Historical Atlas to the Bible. Philadelphia: The Westminster Press, 1945. Revised edition, 1956.

Westminster Study Edition of the Holy Bible. Philadelphia: The Westminster Press, 1948.

Adult Education Association Leadership Pamphlets

Especially helpful pamphlets from Adult Education Association, 1225 19th Street, N.W., Washington, D.C., are these:

No.   1. *How to Lead Discussions,* 1955.

No.   2. *Planning Better Programs,* 1955.

No.   4. *Understanding How Groups Work,* 1956.

No.   5. *How to Teach Adults,* 1956.

No.   6. *How to Use Role Playing and Other Tools for Learning,* 1956.

No.   8. *Training Group Leaders,* 1956.

No. 16. *Training in Human Relations,* 1959.

Audio-Visual Resources

Adult Teaching Series

> Four filmstrips, black and white, 33⅓ rpm. record. Produced by the Methodist Church. Sale, $10.00.

Dynamics of Leadership Series

> Five motion pictures, black and white, 30 minutes each. Produced for National Educational Television. Available from Audio-Visual Center, Indiana University. Rental $5.40 each.

> Titles: "The Anatomy of a Group"; "Individual Motivation and Behavior"; "Diagnosing Group Operation"; "Sharing the Leadership"; "Roadblocks to Communication."

Effective Christian Communication Series

> Four filmstrips, color, textbook, guides, with two 33⅓ rpm. records. Produced by Cathedral Films. Sale, $30.60 set, $7.00 each filmstrip, $3.00 each record.

"Eye of the Beholder"

> Motion picture, black and white, 26 minutes. Produced by Stuart Reynolds Productions. Rental, $25.00.

"Learn a Lot and Like It"

> Filmstrip, black and white, two 12" records, 78 rpm. Produced by Disciples of Christ. Sale, $10.00.

"Members One of Another"

> Filmstrip, color, guide. Produced by United Church Press. Sale, $5.50.

"More Than Words"

> Motion picture, color, 14 minutes. Produced by Henry Strauss and Company. Rental rates vary.

"Roles in a Group"

Filmstrip, color, guide. Produced by the American Lutheran Church. Rental, $2.00.

(Check the *Audio-Visual Resource Guide* for more detailed descriptions of these materials, and for other resources. Most materials suggested are available from denominational audio-visual headquarters, unless other sources are listed in the *Guide*.)

Notes and Acknowledgments

Chapter One

WE LEARN, TOGETHER

1. John Calvin, *Institutes of the Christian Religion,* trans. Henry Beveridge (2 vols.; London: James Clarke & Co., 1949), Bk. III, chap. vi, par. 4.

2. Cf. John Walker Powell, *Education for Maturity* (N. Y.: Hermitage House, 1949), pp. 40-41.

3. *Ibid.,* p. 42. By permission.

4. Reuel L. Howe, *Man's Need and God's Action* (Greenwich, Conn.: Seabury Press, 1953), p. 25. By permission.

5. Marjorie Felder, "Implications of Group Dynamics for a Philosophy of Christian Education" (unpublished Master's Thesis, General Assembly's Training School, Richmond, Va., 1954), p. 57.

6. D. M. Baillie, *God Was in Christ* (N. Y.: Charles Scribner's Sons, 1948), p. 203. By permission of the publishers, Faber and Faber Ltd., London, and Charles Scribner's Sons.

7. *Ibid.,* p. 206.

8. Cf. J. Davis McCaughey, *Study Groups and Their Leadership* (London: SCM Press, 1950), pp. 11-12. By permission.

9. Millar Burrows, *An Outline of Biblical Theology* (Philadelphia: Westminster Press, 1946), p. 248. By permission.

10. Howe, *op. cit.,* pp. 75-76.

11. Ross Snyder, "Group Dynamics in the Life of the Church," *Religious Education,* November-December, 1951, p. 323.

12. *Loc. cit.* By permission.

13. Cf. A. Victor Murray, *Education into Religion* (N. Y.: Harper and Brothers, 1953).

14. *Study Groups and Their Leadership,* p. 9.

15. Cf. David Riesman, *et al., The Lonely Crowd* (N. Y.: Doubleday, 1953. Anchor Books Edition), pp. 302 ff.

16. *Ibid.,* pp. 37-38.

Chapter Two

WE PARTICIPATE, WHILE LEARNING

1. *Planning Better Programs* (Chicago: Adult Education Association of the U.S.A., 1955), pp. 28-29. Drawn by Cissie Peltz. Reprinted from *Adult Leadership,* monthly publication of the Adult Education Association of the U.S.A. Used by permission.

2. *every church and Evanston* (New York: National Council of Churches, 1955), p. 29.

3. *Ibid.,* pp. 27-28.

4. *New Hope for Audiences* (Chicago: National Congress of Parents and Teachers, 1954), p. 12.

5. *Ibid.,* p. 12.

6. *Ibid.,* pp. 15-16.

7. *Ibid.,* p. 16.

8. *Ibid.,* p. 16.

9. Bert and Frances Strauss, *New Ways to Better Meetings* (N. Y.: Viking Press, 1951), p. 80. Copyright 1951 by Bertram W. Strauss and Frances Strauss. Used by permission.

10. Paul Bergevin and Dwight Morris, *A Manual for Discussion Leaders and Participants* (Greenwich, Conn.: The Seabury Press, 1954), p. 66. Used by permission.

Chapter Three

WE STUDY THE BIBLE

1. Alan Richardson, *A Preface to Bible Study* (Philadelphia: Westminster Press, 1944), p. 10. By permission.

2. Suzanne de Dietrich, *Rediscovering the Bible* (Geneva: World's Student Christian Federation, 1942), p. 41. By permission.

3. Nansie A. Blackie, *The Why and How of Group Study* (N. Y.: United Student Christian Council, 1952), p. 21.

4. Bernhard W. Anderson, *Rediscovering the Bible* (N. Y.: Association Press, 1951), p. 22. By permission.

5. Suzanne de Dietrich, *Discovering the Bible* (Nashville, Tenn.: Source Publishers, 1953), p. 4. Adapted from her earlier *Rediscovering the Bible*. Used by permission.

6. *Ibid.,* pp. 4-5.

7. *Ibid.,* p. 34.

8. *Discovering the Bible,* p. 35.

9. Bernhard W. Anderson, *The Unfolding Drama of the Bible* (N. Y.: Association Press, 1953), pp. 57-58. By permission.

10. *Ibid.,* p. 58.

11. *Discovering the Bible,* p. 35.

12. *Ibid.,* pp. 36-37.

13. See especially *How to Enjoy Studying the Bible* (Revised edition, Richmond: John Knox Press, 1946).

14. *Discovering the Bible,* pp. 35-36.

15. Used in several study guides published by the Student Christian Movement of Great Britain.

16. *The Unfolding Drama of the Bible,* p. 57.

17. Personal letter from Mr. Anderson, dated May 27, 1955.

18. J. K. Owen, letter dated March 27, 1955.

19. J. K. Owen, *ibid.*

Chapter Four

GROUP STUDY AND THE CHRISTIAN FELLOWSHIP

1. "Report of Section II, Evangelism," *Evanston Speaks: Reports from the Second Assembly of the World Council of Churches* (New York: World Council of Churches, 1955), p. 20.

2. Paul Maves (ed.), *The Church and Mental Health* (N. Y.: Charles Scribner's Sons, 1953), pp. 93-94. By permission of the publishers.

3. Franklyn Haiman, "The Leader's Role," *How to Lead Discussions* (Chicago: Adult Education Association, 1955), p. 9.

4. "A Message from the Second Assembly of the World Council of Churches," *Evanston Speaks, op. cit.,* p. 9.

5. Some of the overlapping and interrelationship of various types of groups is discussed in Harold W. Freer and Francis B. Hall, *Two or Three Together* (N. Y.: Harper and Brothers, 1954). Emphasis there is on the devotional group.

6. Harry Smith, "Study and the Westminster Fellowship" (unpublished paper used with the Campus Christian Life Section, Presbyterian Educational Association of the South, meeting at Montreat, N. C., June, 1955), pp. 4-5.

7. Cf. *Discovering the Bible,* p. 35.

8. Maves, *op. cit.,* p. 94.

9. *Ibid.,* p. 95.

10. "Report of Section II, Evangelism," *Evanston Speaks, op. cit.,* p. 22.

11. Smith, *op. cit.,* p. 5.

12. Owen, *op. cit.*

13. *A Guide for Curriculum in Christian Education* (Chicago: National Council of Churches, 1955), p. 44.

14. Smith, *op. cit.,* p. 5.